NOMADIC PRESS

OAKLAND

111 FAIRMONT AVENUE
OAKLAND, CA 94611

BROOKLYN

475 KENT AVENUE #302
BROOKLYN, NY 11249

WWW.NOMADICPRESS.ORG

MASTHEAD

FOUNDING AND MANAGING EDITOR
J. K. FOWLER

ASSOCIATE EDITOR
MICHAELA MULLIN

EDITORS
NOELIA CERNA
AQUEILA M. LEWIS-ROSS

CURATORS
TUREEDA MIKELL AND ELENA SERRANO

MISSION STATEMENT

Through publications, events, and active community participation, Nomadic Press collectively weaves together platforms for intentionally marginalized voices to take their rightful place within the world of the written and spoken word. Through our limited means, we are simply attempting to help right the centuries' old violence and silencing that should never have occurred in the first place and build alliances and community partnerships with others who share a collective vision for a future far better than today.

INVITATIONS

Nomadic Press wholeheartedly accepts invitations to read your work during our open reading period every year. To learn more or to extend an invitation, please visit: www.nomadicpress.org/invitations

DISTRIBUTION

Orders by teachers, libraries, trade bookstores, or wholesalers:

Small Press Distribution
1341 Seventh Street
Berkeley, California 94701
spd@spdbooks.org
(510) 524-1668 / (800) 869-7553

PATRICE LUMUMBA: AN ANTHOLOGY OF WRITERS ON BLACK LIBERATION

NOMADIC PRESS + EASTSIDE ARTS ALLIANCE + CALIFORNIA HUMANITIES A STATE OF OPEN MIND

This book was made possible out of a community partnership between Nomadic Press and EastSide Arts Alliance, and by a loving community of chosen family and friends, old and new. Additionally, this project was made possible with support from California Humanities, a non-profit partner of the National Endowment for the Humanities. Visit www.calhum.org.

For author questions or to book a reading at your bookstore, university/school, or alternative establishment, please send an email to info@nomadicpress.org.

Cover artwork: "African American Pi" by John Sims

Book design: Britta Fithian-Zurn

Published by Nomadic Press, 111 Fairmont Ave, Oakland, CA 94611

First printing, 2020

Library of Congress Cataloging-in-Publication Data

Patrice Lumumba: An Anthology of Writers on Black Liberation

p. cm.

Summary: The *Patrice Lumumba* anthology collects the liberatory words of 24 writers, many of whom call Oakland, California, home. Herein are explorations of contemporary colonization, the racial/physical/mental/physic abuses of power, locations of home, alternative modes of work, the health profession, and the healing powers of history. These poems are a call to action for collective change—now.

1. Poetry. 2. Black History. 3. Black Liberation. 4. America General.

LIBRARY OF CONGRESS CONTROL NUMBER: 2020952080

Print ISBN 978-1-7344377-9-9

PATRICE LUMUMBA

AN ANTHOLOGY OF WRITERS ON BLACK LIBERATION

PATRICE LUMUMBA

AN ANTHOLOGY OF WRITERS ON BLACK LIBERATION

NOMADIC PRESS

CONTENTS

PUBLISHER'S NOTE:
FROM EPITAPH TO EPIC/GRAPH

We can and must work backward in our minds to serve a forward purpose. The trope about history's repetition rings completely hollow when real change has not yet occurred. For it is the mattering which is the foremost rhizome. Human condition is a startling experience, and bodies are places at and in which we experience—in fact, they are temples *in deed*: worshipping, shunning, desecrating, remembering; as well as worshipped, shunned, desecrated, and re-membered.

Patrice Lumumba belongs to the whole diaspora now.

TONGO EISEN-MARTIN

Patrice Hemery Lumumba was born under colonial rule in the Belgian Congo in 1925. He was a poet and essayist, a postal worker, a prisoner, a trade unionist, who belonged to the idea of union, not division. He was a pan-Africanist.

Lumumba was a political activist who did not back down, even when lives were at stake—because lives are always at stake. He was a leader who forged ahead for liberation and comm-union.

In 1960, Lumumba became the first Prime Minister of the Democratic Republic of the Congo (then the Republic of the Congo), but only held office for four months before he was forced out and imprisoned. He was then assassinated by firing squad under the direction of the Belgian colonials who were still controlling the new so-called independence.

He was then ... and then ... and then ... Forward to 2020. The extra-judicial *taking* of Black lives is a haunting and happening the world feels and enacts every minute of every day, abroad and at home in the US. Nomadic Press is proud to be involved in this gathering of *giving*, in one volume, filled with Black voices at every decibel.

FOREWORD

A freedom fighter is left for dead inside a voting booth and Californians could use messiah oxygen. City councils promise us that we are in cities and not playgrounds for the corporate hordes. Meanwhile, death is running through our cultural life like a path of least resistance facilitated by late-stage imperialism. In an electrical storm of mugshots, jail profiteering, and extrajudicial killing, they might as well push dollar bills through the holes in our bodies.

Enter the writers.

At the (performance space, archive, organizing haven, and citadel of revolutionary thought, culture, history and practice which is) EastSide Arts Alliance in Oakland, California, we named our writing collective after Patrice Lumumba, the brilliant Congolese protagonist of Afrikan liberation. More specifically, we named ourselves after a picture of him detained on a military truck, captured by imperialist puppets, in maybe the last daylight he would see before being handed over to an imperialist execution. With him there, we make our stand with revolutionary love, struggle, and art.

In front of our children, america is a pathology absorbed. A mob of generational fans of wealth and counterrevolutionaries who damage plenty of the world (even with no skill nor concentration). The ruling class gets drunk on army face paint. The ether and farce of prison reentry; new sects of production/non-production starves our people; begging for a special revolution. While young hearts open to fascism and imperialists try to make bread out of Black people again, passes out spending money to bring down a race; here are poets fit for a Charles White painting, their forearms feeding the multitudes. Moses looking for a sea to scratch.

Here are poems featuring the bravest psyches I've ever known. A maroon community of sorts. Feeling about as much reverence for these ruling class institutions as waiters playing a game of horseshoes out back of a bourgeois hall. Our temper v. Their temper. A blues player with a muddy selflessness chasing a solo all around a room for you, weaving through chairs both empty and filled with ghosts. A Black August throughout the diaspora.

A mayday from us. And when we win, pray that america doesn't return. Live from the victory, we offer this unity of poems.

TONGO EISEN-MARTIN

INTRODUCTION

No Black person, at least up through the twentieth century, gets through life in these United States without paying a fearful Black tax.

ROGER WILKINS, JOURNALIST, HISTORIAN

The writers within the *Patrice Lumumba* anthology address crises of lost and found dignity, Oakland history, memories of protest, police, women on the streets, our purpose, duty, the give up and the get down, the blues, crucial survival tactics, by any means necessary. They evaluate potential loss of womb, mind, family, and body, by bureaucratic epistemic chief-thieves, insisting we give up resisting. Overwhelmed at the helm of a ship we rock and soldier to get over, trapped in prep-positions, folded, creased, in institutions that trigger the need to hide our mind and retreat in colonized dictum's restrictions. Poems fight, defend, teach, reach, and relate, to eviscerate the public masquerade, while we wear our masks. Undercover, through, in between, and around the visceral and political, historical and scientific insights, we connect our circle of life.

These poems catch spells in ways that try to stamp out Black, Brown, Asian, and Indigenous communities. Gentrifying us slowly, insidiously, with teeth smile, brutally, derailing gifts of genetic memory. We take into account how our minds have been gentrified. Denied innate instinct, learning cellular memory that brings wisdom from the other side into reality. Our poems address how institutionalized education provides a forced exodus from our mortal envelopes. Though we make a way out of no way to overcome the shame and trauma. We see and perceive how pimps place blame on poor, houseless, and dissed-ease. How patriarchy subjugates what little is left of the will to live under spells encountered by supremacist ideology. These poems observe two opposing views, infecting in-no-sense with designs that demand cognition not be disturbed when it peaks into Post Traumatic Slave,

Post Traumatic Stress, and Attention Deficit Disorders. Yes, many may need drugs to ease the pain.

There is no discontinuous blood-bone marrow we ride. Rooted to truth from generation to generation, from the other side, we rise. We clarify and remember these poems are a call to action, a collective change, a movement.

TUREEDA MIKELL
CURATOR, WRITER

Now more than ever we must build power for disenfranchised communities and work to address systemic inequities. This is a time for redress and reparations.

In 1999, EastSide Arts Alliance set out to create a Third World Cultural Center to serve and unite the Black, Brown, Asian, and Indigenous communities that compose East Oakland. Our work is in the continuum of the Black Arts Movement and the Xicano Arts Movement. Our work is dedicated to changing the cultural consciousness of this nation. Through the creation and sharing of song, ceremony, dance, music, theater, poetry, posters, murals, and sculptures, we teach each other, build community together, and create new systems of mutual aid. We started a weekly open mic poetry night in 2005, named Holla Back. It was, and remains a way to hear the voices of our community. From this grew the Patrice Lumumba Poetry Workshop, led by Tongo Eisen-Martin. This anthology is the first of what we hope to be many publications co-produced and produced by EastSide Arts Alliance. It is important that we get to be the creators of our own narratives—that Black, Xicano, Asian, and Indigenous folks tell their own stories and present a counter to the mainstream media that gets written about us rather than by us. A key component to our work is our Community

Archives and Resource Project (CARP). This is a collection of over four decades of movement literature, posters, movies, and music recordings. These are the materials we make available to artists and community organizers which provide the history and context that guides their work. This publication will be a part of these living archives.

We have always honored the work of poets—Amiri Baraka was a big part of our founding and ongoing work right up until his passing. Umar Bin Hassan, from the Last Poets, and Sonia Sanchez are both on the EastSide Arts Alliance Advisory Board. Poets issue the clarion call to action. They synthesize the situation and use their powerful voices to touch our souls. The poets gathered here are of that tradition. Read and listen to their words.

ELENA SERRANO

MEMBER OF THE EASTSIDE ARTS ALLIANCE STAFF COLLECTIVE

ALL MY MOTHERS

BY JOY PRIEST

live in an alley
at the back of a lawmaker's mind.

A mind with no imagination

for our reality they say. With teeth
rowed like cigarettes, factory still,

my mothers sweat through a week
of soil on their skin,
unconcerned with grace.

One has grace & a gold tooth,
a tiny heart etched in the middle.

One knows a key ingredient of beauty
is sorrow.

Oven burns cross their wrists.
Fingers calloused from hot plates.
My mother's Marcel curl

every Sunday in the alto section,
her tired face holding down the tenor of

a precarious song. I have

many mothers, you see? Some gone on
but still sitting at the bus stop
as their half-life selves

waiting on the city

to carry them to work.
The jealous mourning dove
holding territory above

the shelter taunts my mothers—

one calls him worse-um,
one has no insurance

& a persistent cough, sitting in the back
of a doctor's mind. She says he has

no imagination to offer. No way out of no way.

She hopes that doctor knows there is no way
to distance ourselves
in a one-room house. My mothers think

these well-to-dos ain't too well.

UNITED

BY JAMES CAGNEY

the tongue as knife, as grenade
the tongue as pilot light to volcano

the tongue as butterfly shrapnel
        spraying radioactive glass

the tongue as battering ram,   axe
        handle, desecrated cross, trigger

the tongue as begging puppy, as monster truck
the tongue Russian neck-tied for a joke

the tongue as assassin: a ninja jingling with blades
        cross-stepping the grassy knoll

the tongue as wooden stake, silver bullet,
        an earthquake with lightning in its hair

the tongue begging kryptonite to freebase

the tongue as apple,   and serpent rolling
        its jellied eggs into the ear

the tongue loaded, unlicensed and steaming
        with cordite, trying to start something

the tongue having kissed every wound
        from inside out is jealous of bone

the tongue has heard of the heart but doesn't
        believe in it—relies on the pulse in dice

the tongue as a wall, a bridge, a gate
        fools gold in moonlight

the tongue tied into a strait-jacket, scatting

the tongue   a lead weight dropped
        onto a garden of peonies—a nest of starlings

the tongue: misfired
                    misplaced
                    misspoke in our last conversation

the tongue blows a hole through its nearest cheek

the tongue thorny and uphill; single bladded
                                        and double barreled

the tongue as museum, snowed in through autumn

the tongue gets it: *yes yes yes*

        but how it loves spitting No.

NO SHAME

BY JENEÉ DARDEN

You aren't the only one fighting this battle
You have nothing to be ashamed of

Your diagnosis does not make you weak
You have nothing to be ashamed of

You can ask for a therapist from your culture or race
You have nothing to be ashamed of

You can request a queer therapist
You have nothing to be ashamed of

If you don't like your therapist, get another one
You have nothing to be ashamed of

1 in 4 people around the world live with mental health challenges
You have nothing to be ashamed of

You need more than prayer to deal with this thing, and that's okay
You have nothing to be ashamed of

Those who tell you to snap out of it, just don't get it
You have nothing to be ashamed of

We live in a sick society that lacks compassion
for people with mental illness
You have nothing to be ashamed of

There's so much going on in the world and in our personal lives
Yeah, it hurts to witness it all
You have nothing to be ashamed of

Don't be hard on yourself
It's not easy, but it's not impossible
You have nothing to be ashamed of

There's so much more to you than your diagnosis
You have nothing,
Absolutely nothing, to be ashamed of

PREPOSITIONS

BY LANDON SMITH

I am only as powerful as the preposition in tow.
I am running either
to
or
from
a pain from which I cannot seem to escape
or evade.
A Patriot Act torture method
        metamorphosed into spyware
        to fulfill voyeuristic fetishes
                of anxiety of black folk
watching black folk
        fighting to make black folk
visible
in an encapsulated red tape
        bureaucracy never made
                to see this hue anyway
unless it's in a memorial service
        filled with prepositions
about
who they were
with
or
what trouble they were fabricated to be
in
or the extension of red tape
from
a casketto
a handcuff

to
a broom
to
the rug our lives are swept
under
until the next preposition tells us which direction
to run
I am tired
I do not have the energy to carry grief, anxiety, and anger
let alone the white guilt
you want me to heave into this mound in need of alleviating—
I am tired.
Tired of being told the Marathon Continues
by people who never cared about Nipsey
before his blood spilled onto the same asphalt
I see in nightmares from a bed I am likely to wake up
from
only to not wake up
in
within Russian Doll cyclical horrors
reliving Breonna Taylor Botham Jean
uncomforting comforter endings
punctuated by my own blood on my own sheets
I am tired
Tired of running into the same justification
built by the same people who felt as entitled
to my body then
as they do now
Hoping to get me to run in the direction of another preposition
just to be locked away
or buried underneath a coarse top soil
or a cement solitary if I run too quickly
into this rage
exploding from the tears running down cheeks
tired of tears running

down cheeks
grieving
another corpse ensconced in red tape
dangling from another participle on another tree
I am tired of running
nowhere.
Tired of preparing to take the innocence from kids
when the day comes that I have to tell them
not to act as carefree as their white friends
since a jail cell has already started being built for them
since
a bullet is already being prepared to be fired
from a squad car for them
since
their mistakes can be fatal and I will never
get to see them again.
Tired of receiving "my heart is sad for you" messages
switching prepositions to position another white person
atop their mound of thoughts and prayers
doing nothing
to dismantle anything
other than guilt felt inside
because the thought of my life left
on concrete means no more Instagram education for free
Tired
of white women with cell phones
Tired
of tear gas Pulitzer photos doused in milk
just to be called powerful
just to have the page flipped
Tired of the prefix "The First Black..."
as reminders exclusion comes at the price of one token
even in hollow celebration of distraction
in an empty Ivy League cloud of derision
of breaking news

Tired
beneath
hallways once home to auction blocks funding tuition costs
for twin beds
in Calhoun Hall
to remind us who agrees that "Slavery [was] a positive good"
Tired of concussions
from breaking through barriers they placed
but sold their presence as God-made
White supremacy is an easy target since it's the biggest target –
Been shooting so long
I have run out of bullets shaped like
my sister's condolences dropped into
a muddy puddle meditation
helpless to find bullets strong enough
to pierce an evil with no heart
to watch me bleed
onto grass to be the First Black
something –
I am another prefix.
First Black poet published.
First Black man to die from the first shot.
First Black poet to die on stage.
First Black poet to publish their own eulogy.
I am tired of these prepositions
weighted with presuppositions
ready to kill us in dreams
only for us to die in our sheets.
I am tired of it
yet it's not even safe to sleep.

TRIGGERS

BY AYODELE NZINGA

i am from the school of
small axes
of the days
when the most violent
write the letter of the law
the law often a faithless mistress
combines to chalk line my boundaries
forgetting who pushed who first
or legitimizing it
complicit in the minefield of my life
enabling the infamous
wearing black robes
white robes
sometimes in scarlet robes
over brooks brothers suits
all the same in their effect
to stones the builder rejects
tethered in halls of injustice
after being dismissed
after planting growing pouring
the foundation
of the crooked house
outside which i sit
fully loaded
rife with triggers
explosive in the conjured myth
informed by action word deed
& the reality of living in the land
of the lawless triggered by reckless lips

using english like a club
toxic ink on cotton
with jim crow's shadow reinventing itself
in the dust of my steps
i got triggers
if i ain't got nothing else
side eye shade interpreted with acuity
fluent in non verbals
subliminals
& lapses in consciousness
& yes you meant that
don't take it back
because you realize
the safety is off
bare reality ain't got filters
i got triggers
can smell the call
will answer it
give you your nightmare without hesitation
i have risen not forgotten
we can get low
i know the steps
wrote some of the songs
you sure you want to sing along
i got triggers
will pull believe that
send you to meet your maker
before i let you send me to mine
i'm a retired slave
been done been unruly
was never suited for oppression
so i stood up
don't try to ride my back
i got triggers
you try to put me on my knees

you find out i squeeze smooth
blow you back to where you come from
have you scratching your life
with your good hand
trying to figure out what comes next
i got triggers
i decipher intention in deed word & text
on the look-out for nappy nets
easily vexed
don't test
i got triggers
lions & gorillas
here
riding in the storm
fully loaded
come for me
i answer the door
if you didn't want
war what you pull up for
reciprocity is a religion
catch me wrong
i serve what i am given
i got triggers

THE CIRCLE

BY TUREEDA MIKELL, STORY MEDICINE WOMAN

For the colonial child, learning became a cerebral activity
and not an emotionally felt experience.
NGUGI WA THIONGO

1989, cool clear vivid afternoon
burden buried 17-years-old breaks in
transports water rippling on shores stings eyes amid
long forgotten pain drawn into a whirlpool
I scream
What's wrong?
What's wrong?
What's wrong?

Shhhhhhh
Spirit says, document this medicine
It isn't all about you
Recall remember reclaim

A veil lifts
I remember being a bio sci. major with a minor in music
Remember trying to connect all subjects into a circle
Remember bacteriology, sociology, physiology, chemistry
religion, anthropology, government, and others
needed connectivity like a circuit keeping the lights on
All arcing off one another

My drive for this covenant superseded my sleep, my dreams

Like an addict, a circle fanatic I needed a fix
though nothing on this campus of higher learning
could demonstrate my theory

My sanity at stake
I remember staring in the bathroom mirror asking

Why do you think like this?
Who does it benefit?
Why are you so entrenched in this reasoning?
What is wrong with you?

One night, studying for three exams
I remember trying to find subjects connective bond, meaning
Reinforce names, measures, formulas, outcomes
Fall asleep
Wake up at 4AM with a migraine telling me

I didn't give you permission to SEE like that!

I remember it would be the first of many migraines
Remember feeding big Pharma my welfare checks to numb headaches

I remember I couldn't let pain get in the way of college
Had to gain knowledge Adam & Eve were thrown out of the garden for acknowledging

Remember the difficulty of chemistry
Its formulas made no sense
Couldn't see the connections
Couldn't link equations visual demands
Couldn't understand professor's lecture until I observe
three African brothers from the continent ace all the exams

I remember getting enough nerve to ask
if I could study with them
Remember how they readily agreed
Remember asking at first home study

How did you master chemistry so easily?

Remember thick West African accent responding

We don't know why they make it so difficult.

Remember another returns

Americans teach subjects in too many different languages.
This creates a weak bond. Disconnects life support systems.

And yet another adds

Chemistry's grams and moles should relate to farming's
pounds and ounces.
In our country, life subjects are whole, not in parts.
If one subject is taken from the whole, it will degenerate
all its parts.

I remember feeling lighter, relieved
Remember chemistry became easier for me
Remember my excitement being able to see
Remember turning in my homework assignments
Professor returns marked wrong.
Remember my African brothers with whom I studied
had no problem

Remember asking the professor

Why did you mark all my answers incorrect?

Remember professor's cold blue eyes answering

Your methods of solving the problems are wrong.

Remember stating

But my answers are correct and
my methods are the same as theirs,
and you didn't mark them wrong.

Pointing to the African brothers hoping for restitution.

I recall... the professor's ...fuck you, Black bitch reply.

They're going back to Africa, you're not.
You need to stick to methods I teach.

I remember his words splitting me in two
I remember thinking who was he to determine
whether I'd go to Africa or not

I remember aphasic shock, couldn't speak
I remember questioning

Didn't we escape mental slavery?

Recall "Lean not on your own understanding" in Proverbs 3:5
Recall "Slaves, obey your masters" in Ephesians 6:5

American Presidents are sworn in on this shit
See holes in institutional mind-yards covered with leaves and grass
My genetic memory hijacked

Recall approaching Ameri-kkk education more cautiously
Recall troubled waters flow off and on all day
Resisting worship of mind-fuck hegemony

Months later
Friend gives me the real "good book" *Muntu*
the African Bantu word meaning *human*
Like the Africans in chemistry said, the book reclaims

> *Seasons, dream time, law, birth, burial, music, art, geology, astronomy, medicine, philosophy, government, agriculture, mathematics, religion, cosmology, and voudoun forms a circle, but to disengage one subject from the circle paralyzes the function of other subjects within the circle*

Is this why migraines nearly paralyzed me?
How many have suffered or are suffering besides me?
I have not had a migraine since *Muntu* reading

Remember Fannie Lou Hamer saying

> *Memory is an insurance policy against loss*

I am Muntu
Hue-man
I recall, remember, and reclaim

Ise olua kule badeo
Our Creator's life will not be destroyed

Ase
And so it is!

DWELLING

BY BRANDON LOGANS

I know that any place I could call home would refuse me.
It would take my flesh and spit me back out.
This was because the place was America.
The land named against its will.
A land my ancestors were brought to against their will.
The idea of home isn't about value.
Value could be reduced to useful,
reduced to commodity,
reduced in the United States to thing.
A thing that is asked to be still, to not breathe more than it has to.

America took every opportunity to uproot a peoples,
        to poison or cut the roots.
They promised us a home if we believed in order.

I knew that there was no home here, because
I was looking for a place the dead could also rest.
I want home to be a kind of loving.
A safe place where you feel satisfied that each day could be your last.
A safe place where you can breathe, where your family can breathe,
where breathing doesn't cause alarm and disgust.

I am desperately trying to find a place to live in - a body?
A home? A future?
I try stripping back skin,
I try to be quivering, red, jeweled.
I no longer trust gestures.
I can no longer relay. Delayed. Helicopters.
Spot light. Hurrying. Steps. Flight.

I was born as motion,
of a curling, of a shell retreat
maneuver to attempt to protect the neck and organs.
I cannot find a home if my flesh is a sweet snack for you,
if my blood is juice for you to quench the economy.

How many poems must I die in to satisfy your thirst?
I am looking for a home to try blooming.
I know it can't be here, but I want it to be.
I want it to be a home for my heart.
My heart, which is family.
My heart, which is community.
My heart who grieves while you kill us in cold blood.
My heart who believes in love.
And what I mean by love, is a belief in a place.
A place I'll call Home, where we live.
Where we live.
Where god dammit we live.

I want to be vulnerable, where vulnerability doesn't mean
a population at risk by the state.
Where vulnerability means alive.
Where vulnerable means No Fear.
Where vulnerable means loving.
A Home not built on any kind of compromise.
A Home that is a future.
A freedom.

KICK DRUM ONLY

BY TONGO EISEN-MARTIN

All street life to a certain extent starts fair

Sometimes with a spiritual memory even
Predawn soul-clap/ your father dying even

Maybe I've pushed the city too far
My sensitivities to landfill districting and
minstrel whistles/ modal gangsterism
White supremacist graffiti on westbound rail
guards
—all overcome and reauthored

revolutionary violence that chose its own protagonists
or muted stage of genius

The garbage is growing voices
Condensed Marxism
for warrior-depressives
Underpasses in their pockets
Because they just might be deities
or decent bid on the Panther name

A merciful Marxism

Disquieted home life
Or metaphor for relaxing next to a person
Who is relaxing next to a gun

I stare at my father for a few seconds
Then return to my upbringing

Return to the souls of Ohio Black folks

Revolution is damn near pagan at this point

You know what the clown wants? The respect of the ant.
Wants to interpret pain only
wants your old soul to turn young
see ancestors in broad daylight
wants to pull a .38 out of a begging bowl
wants me to hurt my hand on this pen

I am not tired of these rooms; just tired of the world that gives them
a relativity

My only change of clothes prosecuted
The government has finally learned how to write poems

shoot-outs that briefly align...
that make up a parable

white bodies are paid well, I posit

do white men actually even have leaders?
all white people are white men

A rat pictures a river
Can almost taste the racial divide
Can almost roll a family member's head into a city hall legislative
chamber

Knows who in this good book will fly

all I do is practice, Lord
I have decided not to talk out of anger ever again

Met my wife at the same time I met new audience members for our pain
We passed each other cigarettes and watched cops win
A city gone uniquely linear
Harlem of the West due a true universe

"I will always remember you in fancy clothes," my wife said
so here I sit... twisting in silk ideation

My rifle made of post-bellum tar
My targets made of an honest language
This San Francisco poetry is how God knows that it is me whining
Writing among the lesser-respected wolves
Lesser-observed militarization
Dixie-less prison bookkeeping/I mean the California gray-coats
are coming
lynch mob gossip and bourgeois debt collection
I mean, it's tempting to change professions mid-poem

in a Chicago briefing, a white sergeant saying, "blank slate for all of us
after this Black organizer is dead."
standard academics toasting two-buck wine at the tank parade

bay of nothing, Lord

nuclear cobblestones, gunline athleticism
and the last of the inherited asthma
children given white dolls to play with and fear
facial expressions borrowed from rich people's shoe strings

I can hear hate
And teach hate
And call tools by people names
And name people dead to themselves

no one getting naturalized except federal agents soon
carving the equator into throats soon

I'm sorry to make you relive all of this, Lord

pre-dawn monarchy
friends putting up politician posters
then snorting the remainder of the paste
minstrel scripts shoveled into the walls by their elders

my children sharpening quarters on the city's edge

For these audiences
I project myself into a ghost like state
For these gangsters, I do the same

every now and then, we take a nervous look east
Sleep becomes Christ
Sleep starts growing a racial identity
do you ever spiral, Lord?
has the gang-age betrayed us?
be patient with my poems, Lord

So much pain
there is a point to crime...

There has to be if race traitors come with it
Lord, is that my revolver in your hand?

Better presidents than these have yawned at cages
Have called us holy slaves
Filled the school libraries with cop documentaries

Baby, I don't have money for food

I have no present moment at all

GEORGE FLOYD

BY HALIMA OLUFEMI

Part of me is like
burn all this shit down!
I really don't care who's doing what,
we'll figure it out later

I hate 'em
Give me a sign
A bullhorn and a gun

Trauma sitting in the back of the squad car
waiting to go take a mugshot but then they take him out

We watched a 10-minute clip of an 8-minute-forty-six-second murder,
a lifetime of pain becoming a catalyst for Black speak by white people
who feel compelled to take to the streets and covertly
        destroy Black things
they're obsessed with destruction and pain and use Black skin
        as a backdrop for they hate

Another part of us died that day

And if it's anything like the last time
When they finish teaching
and raping our revolt

It will be reduced to slaves being put in their place sitting at their countertops begging to be fed with the dogs singing under the threat of water hoses and billy clubs.

Because they think...
if we walked back Black... I mean
uprising Black...

Denmark Vessey, Marcus Garvey, Malcolm X, Black Panthers, Black—

I mean Tulsa, Oklahoma, Rosewood, Florida Harlem Renaissance
we don't need yo shit Black

We'd second line in the middle street and tell them they ain't shit

They leaders ain't shit
They schools ain't shit
They neighborhoods ain't shit

Dig that shit
We don't need this shit

They're afraid... because revenge is their language... we always want
to work it out

Build allies and integrate
Work with nonprofits that pretend like black genius behind white faces
is a new thing
Full-time revolutionary should be more than a title on your
business card

And please don't get me started on politics this shit just don't
work dressed in Black
Feels like they shoved a hand grenade in your mouth, with a gun
to your head and said holla back—when I pull the pin

Black genius stay running toward ignorance and ignorance stay ahead
of the game because they got a hell of a head start and keep recruiting

We get stuck in conversations about how the work should be done with folks on the sidelines who are well intending horrible ass cheerleaders
Start ignoring them or pass them the baton

Because their arguments will have you like them, working concessions distracted by the fans

"Ay, who you rooting for again?

You sound just like this white boy I passed wearin' a MAGA hat yelling Run-Nigga-Run, beside this white girl smiling too gotdamn much, by a deputy Sheriff wearing a white mask with holes in it"

We don't burn crosses; we carry them

To grave sites around our necks
In diamond studded tombs to make sure death protects us before and after we die
A righteous lie… I mean

My life, my life, my life, my life

Is a riot
Is a protest
Is a beautiful contradiction of bullshit
Like the Bible and the Qu'ran or like
Owning black businesses you renting from other people this ain't you shit if you don't own it

And I'm not justifying violence or belittling the sacrifice
I just don't understand how they can expect us to be rational in an irrational place

One minute you had him in handcuffs on the ground
Two minutes your knee bowed on his neck like a devout

Protestant Minister
Three minutes your knee stayed there like a Catholic Priest
during confession
Four minutes he begged for his life
Five minutes he begged for his life again
Six minutes he begged for his momma who been dead for two years...
Seven minutes he went to meet her

Eight minutes and forty-six seconds later
barely got police and dog ass friends for murder

A friend said... We charge genocide again
And again... We charge genocide again
And again... We charge genocide again?

How many ways we gotta die for you to see it

I heard protests don't work but I also heard angry gets shit done; and it might not be liberation but it forced another arrest

So,
until we come up with something else
And they stop killing us
wearing bullet proof vests
I say fuck them and meet us outside for some civil unrest

OH SAY CAN YOU...

BY MELISSA JONES

Our liberation is paused after a nuanced idea
I am a killer of memories that are stolen
Proof that a sword bewildered a programmed mouth
That we stay scripted
Stay?

My backstory: a mother who lost her daughter to greed,
a prostitute that serves drunken men with a fake pussy,
fake titties, fake climaxes, and fake intentions
I know what I don't
And I surround myself in a genre of shit talk,
disaster, and peonies that grow from my cervix

I chew on the wire that sticks out from my ear
Munching and stopping
As I am cut open, the dead leaves die again
And resurface where I left my mouth
There
On a broken wood
A man that never understood
That a mechanical womb serves more than purpose

I beg to be obliterated
And integrated into whatever I am becoming
Whether real or unreal
Nobody can solve me in a time like this
They pour mustard on me and call me appetizer
Dress me in a flower turd

Lift me onto a wrecking board
And draw my structure

Freeze all motor functions

I take back my face
I take back my senses
And begin to feel as multiple casualties surface
in a pool of unmarked arms and digitally glitched irises
It must serve me to stick a needle in a throat
Therapy to rub vaginal fluid on foreheads that never came from me
Marked
Slaughtered
I make my own concoction
earn my own place in this fucked up world

:A POEM ABOUT FIBROID TUMORS

BY ADRIENNE DANYELLE OLIVER

I.

the black woman body carries Afrika
in her womb
and this womb remembers

cargo of bodies
waiting to be crucified
or set free

the body remembers how the strongest cargo
knowing freedom is death
jumped and returned to the ship
as angels
while the deceived
with eyes adjusted to darkness
nose to the smell of despair
cultivate another strength
to pray for the angels to save them
my belly carries
ghosts
a returning
a watching

over corpses
and living bodies—

II.

I learned
to shrink as an accommodation
shoulders
developing knots
from squeezing closed
around lungs
pumping restricted breaths

when the white lady doctor
tells me I need to have
a hysterectomy
I overstand that
what she is really telling me
is this

carried over
in a ship named Good Intent
the body been wearied by this
voyage
and white lady doctor don't understand
how an Afrikan w(omb)und stretched
across the Atlantic and
crucified
can
still bring forth life
can
commune
with
hope

I listen to white lady doctor

read her intentions
and her right to vote
as well intended
                    but know she will never
understand the plight of
                    Mother Afrika to African-American
battered
                    terrorized
                                        dispossessed

tearsinblackboycoffinsandblackgirlchurchbombings/
          turnedbloodintheFergusonstreets
because it's cotton picking season in
MississippiandAlabama/Missouri
Minnesota
Georgia
Texas
and everywhere else

like slave ship my body
carries: life and death
          rotting carnage and breathing captive
suffers: the most damage
knows: "it"—she—the universal black womb is crying out in chorus.

and the white lady doctor's response
is hurried suddenly after 350 years:

rip out the wo(und)mb
toss her out
in a hazardous materials
bag

matter-of-factly she offers black
hat solutions

as if talking to a child
anticipating doves

I have two other options
besides the illusionist's show

one.

I can live with bleeding
bleeding
bleeding
bleeding
blood in the stre/she/ets

two.

I can be cut
with her help have tumors removed
empty the ship in Amerikkka
"land of the free"
and wh/try ignoring the
smell of death
sweep remnants
of clinking shackles
to corners in the
fields of my mind
but
cotton picking season
is year round in
America's soul

and what harm is damaged cargo
in a ship on fire?—
a ship full of cancer
cells
breeding ghosts

still I decide
to dance with the haunted
wo(und)mb on
troubled water.

ON INTERNATIONAL, THE GIRLS ARE ALL LINED UP

BY MIMI TEMPESTT

a body didn't get the world right
a people did
right
right
right on the money that drips maligned between my thighs
right on the street that reveals sanctuary for none
right on the blood i saw hemorrhaged into blue
after my mother gave birth
to another black daughter

right on right
directionless on the path designed for dizzied souls to sell diamonds
demonized by devils
turning tricks until saints

right on wrong

right on "what's wrong?"

right on the breasts that coo conquered alongside kindred feet
in the metropolis black
girls stripped of their emeralds
dancing
dancing
dancing

dying
(we mean) dancing

shhhhhhhh

uuuuuuuuuu

cccccccc

kkk

jjjjjjjjjj

iiiiiiiiii

vvvvvvvvvv

eeeeeeeeee

and shuck and drive
and shuck and lie
and shuck and cry
and shuck and fly
and shuck and play
and shuck and slave
and shuck all night
and shuck and stray

left on the corner of:

the veins the move varicose to the victory of false satiation
left on "who did we lose today?"
left teetering the line of alive and almost always dead
left lapsed on repeat: missing/gone
left as in my daddy [we know how this line fucking ends]
left as in "if i ever catch that nigga in the streets, its gon be _________."
left paying in innocence for the hell they hail, worth dollars
left like the jab that hurled "owned" on my face
left in my body, the drugs that i developed this itch for
left in the closet with my eyes staring lucid into the void

"she was only 15. we made a pact that we would make it out together."

i made it out with wings branded on my back
still they make their lefts on death row
the stolen relics are all lined up
on sale: mouths. hands. youths.
if the price is right,   pussies
always, their souls.

the choir of whores have taken the floor:

he unzipped himself in front of me

they unzip themselves in front of us

and placed the lie that we both know in my mouth

and place the lie we all know in our mouth.

he confessed his demons inside, for a fee

they confess their demons inside, for a fee

until his tiny white angels all flew out

until their tiny white angels all flew out

on international
no angels flewed past me
angels flewed past no me
angels no me flewed past
flewed me
the angels
the angels
(a people)

didn't get the world right

my body
the world didn't get

a people
(the angels)

did get my body

right

right?

THE UNKNOWN BLUES

BY TOLBERT SMALL

Our flutes flew wild beneath the sweet sky of Africa.
Our drums thundered out our victories.
Our harvests grew rich with plantain and papaya.
Our bellies grew fat with our children of love.

Stormy clouds, dark with greed, hovered over our wild paradise.
Butchers of men captured our jungle spirit.
Chained and beaten, they dragged our bones into their death hulls.
Their fat tubas farted shit upon us.
Boxed on shelves, we lay in our own vomit.
With slop for food and piss for a bath, we sailed to your new world.

Your spirit of liberty welcomed us with an auction block.
You stole our mother tongue and then laughed
    as we twisted your English
Your chains squeezed our bones but not our spirit.
Our body submitted but our spirit resisted.
Our resistance grew into the blues

From the "get go," you blessed us with full employment.
Working from dawn to dust, we owned nothing.
Our heart sang out from day to night.
We learned the meaning of the blues as
"The bitter fruits of yesterday bore their bitter weeds today."
We still own nothing.

Beneath the scorched sun, we plowed, chopped, and picked your cotton.
We washed your drawers and ironed your shirts.
We mopped your floors and scoured your knives and forks.

We nursed your babies and washed their asses.
When you were ill, we even washed your ass.
We even mocked our tears over your death.
We bore your children, half slave, half master.
Thus we increased your profits.

In your eyes, the more we slaved; the lazier we became.
To free ourselves from your terror, we escaped into the blues:
"Steal away...
Follow the north star...
No more driver's lash over me...."
You whipped our bodies, poured hot oil into our wounds,
And starved our bellies
We ate your scraps, the crumbs from your table
You raped our women, sold our children;
You even sold your own children.
We wear the mask, smiling on the outside, bitter on the inside.
Our heart sings out the blues:
"Follow the north star...
No more auction blocks over me...."
The fiery blues of freedom burned through our hearts.
Though our bones were chained, our spirit resisted.
Resist we must, our daggers stalked your throat.
As you spit on our food, so we spit on yours.

We broke the chains; we stole away.
With grass for a bed and a rock for a pillow, we struggled northward.
With a scrub bush for an outhouse, we trekked forward.
In our trail of tears, we walked the blues.
We lived the blues,
Death before the driver's lash,
Death before chains,
Death before slavery.

Our weary bones ached for freedom.
Scorched by the sun, numb by the cold, we struggled northward.
With empty stomachs and empty pockets,
Our hearts grew fat with thoughts of freedom.
With dreams of freedom, we escaped into the blues:
        "Steal away...
        Follow the north star...
        Follow the drinking gourd....

Your promised land, the north, greeted us not with a kiss
        But with a slap.
Separate but unequal, Jim Crow laws ruled in the land of the free.
You welcomed us with
        No jobs
        No education
        No health care.
We traded a southern shack for a northern tenement.
Your freedom was a bitter pill to swallow.

Our strange fruit hung from your trees.
In the land of the free, you denied us the right to vote.
In the land of the free, we shuffled through your back doors.
In the land of the free, we set in the back of your buses.
Your promised land turned heaven into hell.
        We ran your factories.
        We scrubbed your floors.
        We scoured your dishes,
Such was the promised land.

During the great wars, our red blood bled for your liberty.
We fought violently for your cause;
Yet we fought nonviolently for our cause.
You embraced our non-violence,
As you spread violence throughout the world.

Our struggles opened the door not only for our people,
But also for women,

For red, yellow, and other people of color.
Yet with the door open, we still did not share in the feast
        From your table.
We still fight over your crumbs.

Our heart soars.
Our horns scream.
Our drums thunder.
Our pianos bark.
We sing out the blues;
The blues lost and buried in our heart.

PLATITUDES

BY SARAH DUDZIC IYER

what doesn't break you
sometimes
bends you
folds you
at the creases
again and again
til you are
worn so thin
you will tear
if you are turned too fast
what doesn't break you
wrings and picks at you
like a tissue
in an old woman's coat pocket
damp and disintegrating
what doesn't break you
is sometimes a withering
is drenched and swollen
and blue and barely -
what doesn't break you
forgets you sometimes
and you wonder if
you'll disappear entirely
when you fall away from
the lips and flickering mind screens of
everyone who has ever loved you
until you fade like a word
on a page in the sun

what doesn't break you
can rub you into dust

THAT TIME MY 5TH PERIOD CLASS FOOLED A FALSE GOD

BY MEILANI CLAY

thought if i stayed in the tree
i could somehow put out the fire

lobotomized my pedagogy
colonized my curriculum
tired mouths shout
feed me
but i've been starved, too
under scrutiny   stern tutelage
            (like generations of sparrows before me
            regurgitating hope and resilience
            under a watchful eye)

i wept every Sunday

prostrate and pleading before a merciless god
            (bureaucracy, a vapid olympian
            come down from the clouds
            attempting to wear one of us for a mask)

i fed them what i could
as swiftly as i grasped annelid awareness
i found it spewing from my mouth
hastily digested   missing segments
still, it nourished
my best did
on my worst days

i said i love you and meant it
made sure they ate
used words instead of fists
            (even if the words were
            yo, for real, fuck you)
better that than bleeding nose

once, under threat of discovery
buzzard in my ear   judging the distance between us all
no one made a peep   put lead to paper
watched me   flit   around them watching

after i earned a thumbs up
from the vulture coaching me on classroom culture
            (or, clearing a cleaner culvert into incarceration's ditches)
i heard
                        so they believed us
and i swear i could have burst into song

THE MOMENT I REALIZED

BY DAJAUN CARTER-WOODARD

Blood has a tendency to drip slowly/
The metallic taste is undeniably familiar/
The hunk of flesh hanging is exposed in the night breeze,
    gives it a minty chill/
This was the night I learned that physical wounds can heal better
    than emotional ones/
The feeling I had when those lights flashed behind me/
Those bright cherries and blueberries/
Was almost the equivalent of seeing a tiger prowling/
The adrenaline in my frontal cortex was racing at full speed/
The encounter was deafening/
Especially after the first blow/
Handcuffed, a struggle to find shelter from the raining fists/
Senses fully aware, although I wish they wouldn't be/
I can still smell the gloves the officer wore/
How he asked me questions he physically restrained me from answering/
The grip around my throat crushing any chances of words escaping/
Being noncompliant, I fall victim to the rabbit punch/
Cries for help stolen in the wind/
Screaming for help seems useless when the perpetrator
    is the protection as well/
And a gesture of mercy, you uncuff us and leave us to tend to our
    own wounds/
Two of us/
Six of y'all/
And, I was only 16/
This was the moment I realized you were the enemy/
This fear and hatred is a cocktail so toxic I would not wish
    on my worst enemy/

Don't tell me how we need police if you cannot tell me
their point of origin/
Why the officers were once overseers of slaves?/
And have for so many years they overlooked/
Friday nights like these/
Being a Black man in America, we fall victim to you repeat offenders/
The steel bar from your Nigger beater 2000/
That sent electricity to my head although I was hit in my leg/
The worst part of being pepper sprayed is reliving the moment
in the shower/
Trying to wash it out of your hair/
The moments I see my kids crying as you place me in the back
of the squad car/
This was only supposed to be a simple trip to get Chinese food/
The fact my 15 year old sister started her period/
The day you kicked my mother's door down/
Which you also refused to replace/
Placing this terrified minor in shackles only to make no arrests/
Yes/
You are the enemy/
I noticed how blood has a tendency to drip slowly/
And this metallic taste of blood is way too familiar/
These physical wounds heal/
But these mental scars/
The built-up cortisol in my system/
Which may kill me anyway/
Hypertension runs rampant in the Black community/
PTSD comes more frequently than school supplies or fresh food
for our children/
When we sit our kids down for the "TALK"/
It's not about the birds and the bees/
But those cherries and blueberries/
What would life be like without police?/
For me in particular/
The world will be a safer place/

FEED

BY DEE ALLEN

This ain't no charity!
This is a protest!

Supermarkets, hotels,
Eateries, coffeeshops
Make waste out of fresh & prepared
Food, tonnes, at day's end!

This ain't no church function!
This is a protest!

Bullets, assault rifle, tanks,
Aeroplanes, destroyer ships, bombs
Make far-away lands killing fields!
National budget spent mostly on this, forget homes!

This ain't no city programme!
This is a protest!

Hunger tends to exist
In the First World, too!
So food is recovered
From rotting as waste!

This ain't no welfare line!
This is a protest!

Ongoing against military build-up,
Gearing up for war, nights and days

Dining from empty plates, drinking from empty cups,
Sleeping on empty bellies, dreaming of a decent meal!

Revolution sometimes begins from
The bottom of a bowl!

Public space gets reclaimed!
That space becomes inclusive!
Fresh, prepared, free
Vegetarian food is shared with neighbours!

Afterwards, workers & poor alike leave
The corner with fuller bellies.
Hunger is much worse on the streets!
So some do what class society fails to do:

Feed the people!
Food to every fork!

This ain't no charity!
This is a protest!

SIREINES RISING

BY ALIE JONES

I don't want to remember my life before mermaids.
I was raised by saltwater Queens.
Blessed by magical beings of mythic proportions.
Daughters of Yemaya and Gumbo.
Those who remind me of the beautiful resilience that lives within us.
Coiled crowns adorned with Cowrie.
Goddesses, who maintain the grace of a gazelle with the ever changing tides.
Mes Sireines, My Mermaid Queens;
flowing,
        crashing,
                  rising.

My grandma Genevieve,
Cayenne pepper royalty.
Celestial matriarch.
Soft, yet steady as a metronome in the kitchen.
With a laugh that could brighten any dim room.
Unafraid of what is to come because her certainty is founded in love.
Her setbacks created the beginning of her greatest comebacks.
Flowing through the roughest currents and remaining strong;
flowing,
        crashing,
                  rising.

Mother Theresa,
Calming like rosemary and gentle as gardenias.
Earth Warrior who taught me to respect and protect the earth.
To value all forms of life.

Holding space for her softness and her offspring,
Unconditionally magical, conjuring potions that transformed the flu
        into a slight sniffle,
Or inventing the perfect bedtime story.
She grew in the midst of adversity.
Never allowing fear to stop her pursuit.
Crashing against every judgment or expectation with determination;
flowing,
        crashing,
                rising.

Mes Sireines, My Mermaid Queens;
Cousins, who always remind me that I could do anything.
Sisters, that challenge me to seek softness in times of pain and trauma.
To look at myself in a mirror, untarnished by self loathing.
My aquatic angels, who kept me sane when I thought all I ever could be was crazy.
Loving with hearts wide open.
Guided by our gut feelings and our star signs.
Rêveurs, croyants, amants, et guerriers.
Dreamers, believers, lovers, and warriors.
Rising above black holes of doubt, insecurities, and fear;
flowing,
        crashing,
                rising.

DIRECTION OF TRUTH

BY LYNSIE FALCO

air and water
unstoppable
flow with clarity
in the direction of truth
to the home of breathing words
of the unforgotten
some gone
all resurrected

Octavia Butler
spaceships ahead
time travel a galaxy
redirection
conviction in river current,
a healing and uncovering

loss like a universe
brightness of stars cherished
in the depth of night
to see Her,
Say Her Name,
so deserving of life and love,
Sacred

run fingers along pages
let wind rush over skin
in the direction of truth
root to Earthseed
breathe titles,
surrounding phrases like

embraces refuge
Ms. Morrison says in order to fly,
here's what to do

She has written it down
permanently,
unafraid of Her own name
She who heals,
anyway

She is thunderous
She is change
Her spirit never in vain,
wisdom flows out from
Her watering imagination,
creation comes from within
divine ebb and flow

Brathwaite knows the rhythm
of the wave, tidalectic
deepest Deities
ocean spirituality
despite painful interruption
of history
an after-life
Edwidge Danticat describes
healing underwater, under sea
one year the soul rests there before rising free

testimony
home of
breathing words
unstoppable
like air and water
flow
in the direction of truth

CLARITY

BY SARAI BORDEAUX

We are what perfection wishes it could be. Free.
Rough around the edges, wild in the eyes.
We are not just our Ancestors Dreams
We.

Their most vivid and lucid distillations
Their reflexes, the hairs that stood up on their arms
Their deepest breaths,
Their belly laughs,
We are a part of them as they are apart of Us.
Shimmering.

We together are magic.
When we remember our Joy, we are Powerful.
When we know Our Story, we are
Golden, deep, Unending.
Like our skin in the Sun.
We are the waters, troubled and troubling
Resisting.
Still we ride this wave.
Break open like seeds that extend roots into the dirt.
The dirt that still contains the blood stolen from us,
The soil made so rich with that blood it holds
Every Instance.
Every Universe.
Everything perfection wishes it could be.

TEST

BY QR HAND, JR.

The sun is the only thing warm
As hearts are in freezers to keep
Well   not enough for a real
Smorgasbord any more   limbs
And   eyes only now   and   they
Throw a way any thing over 7
As stiff with age   trying to invent
Televisions with out commercials
Buying time   stealing from laundromat

Washers   and   dryers   paying off tiny
Look outs with collected roaches skimmed
From neighbor hood vipers   and   their
Often visitors pointed out by the tiny ones
As if that's what they were born for   like
Chimney sweeps in a dingy dicken's tale
So terrible competing against brothers   and

Sisters to stay small   and   not be eaten
Having fewer birth days   putting candle makers
In to a precarity zone   and   the few basket ballers remaining
Had to accept small pensions   or   smaller cells

In the older walls be tween the reservations   so
Ecologically sound

And   financially responsible   where the will
To power's in a world of trouble   some   or all
Or   in the hall ways of that large apartment
At 112th street   and   7th avenue   across the street
From a little hotel   mortal   metal   medals   for
Valorous behaviors in the service of cosmetic prosthetics
For

Returnees of foreign wars who could no longer be
Hidden in zoos   and   circuses for the criminally insane
From the previous wars of valor   mortal metal   and
Honors for academics too old   or   sub versives   whose
Protesting often led to blood curdling screams   in future

Protests in the court of too late for you   and   yours
If you got any yours left   and   then there's this
Dreary expiation   ain't the California I moved to
So much more blood flooding the plain than raining
Which gotta be pumped back   and   forth   and
In   and   out fuckin' travesty of water ways

Weighs a lot on all those draft dodgin' farmers
Lazy on the land   the very frumiousness of it
No longer just banter snatched in to a vortex   of

Meanings colliding on receding ideological tramps   and
Their directress   and   that distress at the redressology
Of it insufficient heft

They all said your draw bridge is down for
The clowns   and   farmers to cry in the streets
Teeming now flesh flood didn't come to California for
The rain   but   it's said this very earth needs it   if
They're gonna continue to make wars here   killing
As many possums as possible

Real   or   just playin' possum's a good enough kill
In some counties   (lithe mettle there now   bright
Sun up morning beams   bright poems wending centuries a
Way like a saxophone solo in sweet jungle time(s)   and
Covering the tons of tripe they try to stuff drummers

With   speaking dreams   and   a fuller tongue   with
No words   and   vital sounds past   and   (i)   all ways
Wanted to stay on the earth   feet there   and   finding
Spirit in soil   eschewing the high in a sky I knew not   and
not to care for   but   in

A loving family   existing in such tensions   impacted beyond
Words it had stopped working   like constipations do a strike
In the harbor   hopes in be low deck   and   sit there
An operation going In after it   wearing so many hats

Determined   to my shit   your life   they say loud

First little break comes   then hoping   making the profound
Simple   yet heady   ducats for buckets   takin' it to the streets
All over the world   falling down   progressions   posters' high brio
And   lots of bottles   bruja   and   hubbub   a pun fight   at
An o.g. joint   hidden from draft boards

THE ATHENIAN NILE CLUB OAKLAND, CALIFORNIA

BY JOAN TARIKA LEWIS

Geoffrey's Inner Circle, located at 410 14th Street in Oakland, California, is the largest Black-owned nightclub and historic institution on the West Coast. Mr. Geoffrey Pete is a legend in Oakland, son of Mr. Herman Pete and Dorothy Reid Pete, descendants of early California pioneering families. Mr. Pete is not only a prominent businessman, he is founder of the *Niagara Democratic Club*, philanthropist, supports small businesses, musicians, artists, and youth programs. Mr. Pete does not stop there—he gathers community volunteers and churchgoers to cook, serve, and feed hundreds of unsheltered each and every holiday.

To understand the significance of *Geoffrey's Inner Circle* is to examine Africa's story, our-story, and his-story. Why is this important and what does this have to do with *Geoffrey's Inner Circle*? Tradition, tradition, tradition! *Geoffrey's Inner Circle* was previously owned and operated by one of the Bay Area's largest all-white male exclusive private membership club, *The Athenian Nile Club*—a club where politicians and power brokers closed back room deals over handshakes and three-martini lunches. *The Athenian Nile Club* was a merger of the *Athenian* and the *Nile Club*, April 28, 1915, with a membership of six-hundred-and-seven members. The social club provided its membership with an interior modeled to resemble the African Temple of Ausar (Osiris). The African Egyptian theme inspired the naming of the club. Its members were composed of prominent professional Oakland businessmen. The formation of the *Athenian Club* followed a tradition long observed in Europe and notably in the US— members sworn to secrecy. Social affiliation existed in Greek and Roman times and, in modified form, continued through the guilds in the Middle Ages.

Early southern European invasions into northern Africa encountered a civilization already centuries old while Europe was still in its infancy. Greek writers like Plato and Herodotos wrote testimonies about the highly cultured Black Africans living along the Nile. They also acknowledged the Greek debt to Egypt. Our noted historians, Dr. John Henrik Clarke, Dr. Asa Hilliard, Dr. Theophile Obenga, and Dr. Ben Jochanan's primary research is published in numerous books, publications, essays, and lectures. In 1974, Senegalese Dr. Chiek Anta Diop and Dr. Theophile Obenga successfully challenged UNESCO, proving scientifically that the ancient Kemites were indeed Black Africans. The Africans called the land Kemet, meaning Black people of the black earth. They named cities like Ta-Seti, Meroe, Puanit, Kush, Numidia, Khart-Haddas, and Summer. Around 300 B. C., foreign invaders changed the name of Kemet to Egypt.

The Kemites created entire universities and libraries filled with their interpretations on the fundamental teachings of salvation. The Medu Netcher, or sacred texts, represented their original and authentic philosophical speculations on life and death, truth and justice, social order and chaos, happiness in eternity, speculating the beyond, and emergence of matter. These were papyrus scrolls documenting Sirius B star system, astronomy, literature, architecture, sciences, biology, psychology, medicine, ethics, and mathematics. African artisans and craftsmen had strict standards and a long tradition of furniture making, smelting, navigation, geology, metallurgy, theater, agriculture, sculpture, engineering, and wrestling. The same musical instruments created during this period still exist today. A rich unified culture, with traditions nurtured for thousands of years, are documented by dynastic genealogies carved into stone, painted upon the walls and ceilings—visual reminders and edification. When it came to constructing buildings, African architects created colonnaded lotus pillars, which were prototypes for Greek doric and corinthian pillars. Every building of importance has pillars, whether it is a courthouse, city hall, library, church, or in Oakland's *Athenian Nile Club*. In America, Benjamin Banneker was commissioned to design the capital of the United

States in Washington, D.C., with the symbol of resurrection, and the Washington Monument resembling the Kemetic obelisk. Building designs reflecting 18th-dynasty mortuary temples, Kemetic symbols and writings. The statue of Abraham Lincoln was designed in the spirit of the African engineers that constructed statues of their pharaohs. Even the hairstyle of President George Washington favored the headpiece of the Sphinx.

The young city of Oakland was no exception. By 1881, with a population of only 34,555, there were six major Masonic Lodges, two chapters of Royal Arch Masons, and one chapter of Eastern Star. The International Order of Odd Fellows, the Druids, Knights of Pythias, Red Men, Hibernians, Good Templars, B'nai B'rith, Orangemen, Foresters, Herman Sons, Ancient Order of United Workmen, Knights of Honor, American Legion of Honor, Society of Chosen Friends, Patriotic Sons of America, Native Sons, and Freemen's Brotherhood were also in existence. The notion of gathering of people into social and professional organizations represented to them an important force.

As Oakland built its economic base, gentlemen's social clubs sprang up around its downtown. *The Athenian Club* was built April 14, 1883, organized in Oakland September 26, 1896. A second club, *Athenian and Nile*, co-existed in Oakland for close to nineteen years. By 1915, the two clubs merged to form one large club equal to the prestigious *San Francisco Bohemian Club.*

West Oakland, by the 1930's–1950's, established a thriving Black community and economic base of its own. Among the many organizations were the Athens Elks Lodge No 70, Cooperative Hall Association, Hospitality House for Servicemen, K of P Marchimel, Masonic Temple F & AM, Art and Industrial, Berkeley Civic, Booker T Mothers, Book Lovers Society, Campus Improvement, Civic Breakfast Study Club, Cosmos Social Club, Diners Car Cooks and Waiters Union, Acorn, East Oakland Improvement, and Marcus Garvey's UNIA. To them, "the great river of life was the basic source of life-sustaining water." It became an object of worship and deep appreciation.

A phrase that was often recited at *Athenian Nile Club* events:

Adoration to the Nile!
Hail to thee, O Nile!
Who manifests thyself over this land Who cometh to give life to Egypt!
Mysterious is thy issuing forth from darkness On this day wherein it is celebrated! Watering the orchards created by Ra,
To cause all the cattle to live
Thou givest the earth to drink,
O inexhaustible one Loving the fruits of Sebet
and the first fruits of Aapera
Thou causest the workshops of Ptah to prosper.

Mr. Geoffrey Pete purchased the club in 1993 when the aged and dwindling membership of the once affluent *Athenian Nile Club* decided to sell it. The building was the best-kept secret in Oakland. After ascending the stairs at 411 14th Street, one encounters a 4' x 6' painting representing Horem-aket (the Sphinx); then, a colonnaded entry room, with grand piano, lounge room, library, billiard room, plush carpet, and turn of the century wood and brass bar.

The bar was brought from the Bankers Restaurant San Francisco bistro. It traveled across the Bay to the Club's present location after extensive use during the 1915 World's Fair in San Francisco. When the sideboard room was remodeled in 1951, many obsolete fixtures were removed, but the back bar was renovated and provided a place of prominence.

Architect Walter J. Mathews designed and supervised the construction of the building—elegant, graceful and functional. Built to last for decades. If only those walls could talk, what secrets they would reveal. After acquiring the building, Mr. Pete found hidden photographs of the *Athenian Nile's* past traditions. To celebrate its 70th Anniversary party in 1953, *Athenian Nile Club* hosted a sumptuous dinner and minstrel show—yes, a minstrel show. Its members were entertained by musicians and singers dressed up in black face. The event was held in the ballroom, complete with a 6' x 10' slice of watermelon that served as the stage backdrop. The event was directed by Mildred Lane Barr, Oakland City Attorney Hilton Melby M.C., and Lyule Vincent musical soloist. Present were the board of governors of the ANC, Harvey H. Bechtel, Bauer Kramer, Harold Lorentzen, M.F. Hallmark, James Freeman, and John O'Shea.

The new *Geoffrey's Inner Circle* has entertainment of a different sort. Attracting greats like Wynton Marsalis, Muhammad Ali, Ron Dellums, Jerry Rice, Willie Brown, Betty Soskins, Michael Jordan, Kamala Harris, Ruth Bechford, John Burris, Janis Maxie Reid, Attn John Burris, Maya Angelou, Runoko Rashidi, Richard Gant, Phyllis Hyman, and LL Cool J. The club's first musical ensemble was a jazz band named Ta-Seti, organized by Geoffrey's cousin, violinist Joan Tarika Lewis. The band included Mondre Moffett (flugelhorn), Paul Smith (drums), bassist Ron Belcher, George Spencer (piano), and Baba Tunde (percussion). The band was named in honor of a city along the Nile river. There is always a surprise musical guest gracing the stage with all forms of African American music: Jazz, Blues, Gospel, R&B, ole school, new school, and comedians; contemporary music with Yancey Taylor, Calvin Keys, Faye Carroll, Darlene Coleman, Marcus Shelby, Rhonda Benin, NBA Champions, the best Chefs in the Bay Area. The club also hosted birthday parties, lectures, weddings, anniversaries, community events, conventions, and all types of celebrations in an atmosphere of happiness, safety, and good times.

Joyce Gordon Gallery is located downstairs and hosts art exhibitions and artist talks showcasing local and national creative Black artists. Mr. Geoffrey Pete has successfully preserved an important institution for Oakland where all are welcomed and treated hospitably and with respect. Thank you, Geoffrey Pete, for all your hard work and dedication. Thank you for building an institution we are very proud of and will enjoy for decades to come.

In the name of friendship, good will, progress, peace, and prosperity, congratulations Mr. Pete. Long live *Geoffrey's Inner Circle.*

Geoffrey's Inner Circle is located at 410 14th St., Oakland, California 94612, info@geoffreyslive.com

This paper is dedicated to Mr. Geoffrey Pete, family, musicians, artists, patrons, and community, as well as Oakland's own writer and poet laureate, Ms. Tureeda Mikell.

ACKNOWLEDGEMENTS

Nomadic Press and EastSide Arts Alliance are deeply honored to be in partnership on our first (of what we hope are many) community collaborative publications to be published in the future.

Innumerable thanks to Tureeda Mikell, for organizing and collecting works for this anthology, and the stellar lineup of writers and poets who consented to have their work help heal communities everywhere. They offer blood, sweat, and tears here, laying out blood-lines that seep into concrete—hope with new scope for a better tomorrow.

Special thanks to Tongo Eisen-Martin for his presence and assistance in reaching out to, and pulling in, collaborative communities that share *our* word's concerns for the devastating times we are witnessing. His ability to expose poets to Bowery Poetry Club/BAS, Urban Word in NYC, to San Francisco Cultural Heritage, S.F. Jazz Festivals, S.F. State, Mission Cultural Arts Festivals, and beyond is a journey we continue to share. Special thanks to Don Juan-Carter for being the host of "Holla Back" for all these years.

And very special thanks to J. K. Fowler, publisher of Nomadic Press, and Michaela Mullin, Associate Editor of Nomadic Press, for all of their detailed assistance in making this an outstanding anthology and inviting John Sims, the cover artist, into this project. We are so thankful that he agreed to have his profoundly provocative art displayed on the cover of this book.

CLASSROOM GUIDE

DEAR READER,

Please use this cultural fire to keep you warm and shed light on your dark nights. Take time to address the critical thinking skills we use for survival—what our mothers had to bear living in the city, sharing one room with her children, half alive. Or the young girls, trying to keep a roof and get food, walking international streets. What of damaged wombs, shame, tongues as weapons, drums, triggers, the circle, the prepositions that drive under, over, and with, to wear us out. Think about how we learn through the colonial lens—back stories, Black stories, obliterated. Current stories, too, make a moment that realizes the world would be a safer place for many without police. Sustenance is necessary. Not guns. Not bombs. Not wars.

Yet we navigate the holes and insecurities, like air and water moving through and around at will, our truth, elusive, like black matter. We are grateful, though troubled. We both resist and remember where we come from.

Below are some of the main themes and questions that thread through this anthology, with a few representative poems for each.

1. **Racial, physical, mental, and psychic abuses of power on people of color**

    - George Floyd
    - The Circle
    - The Moment I Realized

2. **People are often forced to act outside their nature in order to make a living**

- On International The Girls Are Lined Up
- That Time
- Unknown Blues

3. **Health profession and ownership of mind/body/judgments**

- Fibroid Tumors
- No Shame
- Platitudes

4. **Contemporary colonization and its cohorts**

- Kick Drum Only
- Feed
- Oh Say Can You...

5. **The effects that institutionalized racism has on the education of students of color**

- The Circle
- That Time
- Preposition

6. **What should we call home?**

- All My Mothers
- Direction of Truth
- Dwelling

7. **Critical thought, place, and prepping our positions**

    - Preposition
    - Triggers
    - United

8. **Clarity and healing of history**

    - Athenian Nile Club, Oakland, California
    - Clarity
    - Sireines Rising

DEE ALLEN

African-Italian performance poet based in Oakland, California. He has been active on the creative writing & Spoken Word tips since the early 1990's. He is the author of five books: *Boneyard, Unwritten Law, Stormwater,* and *Skeletal Black*, all from POOR Press. His newest from Conviction 2 Change Publishing, *Elohi Unitsi* and 28 anthology, including *Your Golden Sun Still Shines, Rise, Extreme, The Land Lives Forever, Civil Liberties United, Trees In A Garden Of Ashes* and the newest, *Colossus: Home*, are under his figurative belt so far.

SARAI BORDEAUX

is from California. She enjoys watching sunsets and lizards and has just finished her Masters Degree from SFSU in Education with an emphasis in Equity and Social Justice.

JAMES CAGNEY

Oakland native James Cagney is the author of *Black Steel Magnolias In The Hour of Chaos Theory*, winner of the PEN Oakland 2019 Josephine Miles award. Visit nomadicpress.org/store for his book, and find more of his writing at TheDirtyRat.blog

DAJUAN CARTER-WOODARD

Oakland Native. Father Son Teacher Revolutionary Poetry is the lens I view the world in.

MEILANI CLAY

is an educator, mama, and writer from Oakland, California. A graduate of Howard University and the University of San Francisco's Urban Education and Social Justice program, Meilani bridges worlds with her words and aspires to build forts out of books written by Black women.

JENEÉ DARDEN

is an award-winning journalist, public speaker, mental health advocate and proud Oakland native. She hosts KALW's arts segment Sights & Sounds and is their East Oakland reporter. Jeneé blogs at CocoaFly.com and is the author of *When a Purple Rose Blooms*, a womanist collection of poems and essays out with Nomadic Press.

SARAH DUDZIC IYER

is a New York-born, Jersey-raised musician and writer who lives near Richmond, California. Most of her writing has been in song form and her current band, lay/lie released its second album, *The Long Road From the Desert to the Sea,* in May 2020. She is grateful for the opportunity to revive her love of poetry writing at the feet of giants in the Hollaback Poets Circle.

TONGO EISEN-MARTIN

Originally from San Francisco, Tongo Eisen-Martin is a poet, movement worker, and educator. His latest curriculum on extrajudicial killing of Black people, We Charge Genocide Again, has been used as an educational and organizing tool throughout the country. His book titled, "Someone's Dead Already" was nominated for a California Book Award. His latest book "Heaven Is All Goodbyes" was published by the City Lights Pocket Poets series, was shortlisted for the Griffin Poetry Prize and won a California Book Award and an American Book Award.

LYNSIE FALCO

is an educator and poet who believes poetry is a matter of the spirit. She is grateful for lasting community, truth, and love from Oakland. Lynsie currently resides with her partner in Xiamen, China.

QR HAND, JR.

was born in Brooklyn, New York, in 1937. He is the author of three poetry books, *i speak to the poet in man* (jukebox press, 1985), *how sweet it is* (Zeitgeist Press, 1996), and *whose really blues, new & selected poems* (Taurean Horn Press, 2007). His next book *Out is Nothing* will be published by Black Freighter Press.

ALIE JONES

is a self-care advocate, writer, artist, and Creole mermaid. She is passionate about promoting mental health awareness, body positivity, and engaging in new conversations through the arts.

MELISSA JONES

Born and raised in Oakland, California, Melissa Jones is a singer-songwriter and poet. She is an author of two poetry collections, *Pineapple Grenades* and *Black Girl Mango Seeds*. Themes of Black womanhood, Black culture, and self love from trauma are recurring themes in her work. As she continues her artistic journey, she hopes to continue to experiment, innovate, and inspire others through her work.

JOAN TARIKA LEWIS

Visual artist, jazz violinist, genealogy researcher, creator of MudCloth Magical Puppet Theater, Co-Director of Oakland Spirit Orchestra, art workshop facilitator, Black Panther Party alumni, Oakland historical and Black Power tour guide and lecturer. Fine Art exhibitions include TheBlackWomanIsGod at SOMA Gallery, YBCA, Joyce Gordon Gallery.

BRANDON LOGANS

is a poet from Oakland, California. He has his M.F.A in Poetry from Mills College. If he had to try to describe himself succinctly, he is a rectangular sheet of honey 30" x 62", 6" above any surface.

TUREEDA MIKELL

Hell bent on asserting life, activist for holism, is an educator, griot, poet, story medicine woman, and QiGong healer. She is founder of the Tree of Life Foundation, H. L. P., has published over 70 student anthologies written by at-risk youth via California Poets in the Schools since 1989. Her full collection, *Synchronicity: The Oracle of Sun Medicine,* was published by Oakland-based Nomadic Press in 2020.

AYODELE NZINGA

Ayodele Nzinga is the founding producing director of the Lower Bottom Playaz. She is the founding Director of the Black Arts Movement Business District Community Development Corporation, Oakland, (BAMBD CDC). Nzinga holds an MFA in Writing and Consciousness, and a Ph.D. in Transformative Learning. Work for the page includes

SorrowLand Oracle and *The Horse Eaters* (both published by Nomadic Press), *A Narrative Inquiry into Performance Pedagogy*, work in *Vision Magazine*, two volumes of the *Journal of Pan African Studies*, *14 Hills Journal*, *Magnolia Journal*, and in the anthologies, *Environmental Terrorist*, and *Say it Loud*. Nzinga is a Cal-Shakes Artist Investigator Alumni, a Helen Crocker Russell Arts Leadership Fellow, and a member of the Alameda County Women's Hall of Fame. She is recognized by the August Wilson House as the only director in the world to direct the complete August Wilson Century Cycle in chronological order.

ADRIENNE DANYELLE OLIVER

is a poet-educator, hip-hop scholar from Little Rock, AR living in the SF Bay Area. Her work explores healing from diasporic displacement and has appeared in *Storytelling, Self & Society* (Wayne State University Press 2018), The San Francisco Museum of the African Diaspora's (MOAD) poet corner, and *Split This Rock*'s virtual open mic. Some of her favorite authors include Zora Neale Hurston and Tyembia Jess, among many others. When not writing, Adrienne is watching documentaries and leads a monthly healing writing circle for Black women.

HALIMA OLUFEMI

My name is Halima J. Olufemi and I was born and raised in Jackson, Mississippi. I am a member of the Malcolm X Grassroots Movement, JXN People's Assembly, and work with the People's Advocacy Institute around their Participatory Defense Program. My work is deeply rooted in the total liberation of Black people.

JOY PRIEST

is the author of *HORSEPOWER* (Pitt Poetry Series, 2020), winner of the Donald Hall Prize for Poetry. She is the recipient of the 2020 Stanley Kunitz Prize and her work has appeared or is forthcoming in the Academy of American Poets' *Poem-a-Day*, *APR*, *The Atlantic*, *Poetry Northwest*, and *Poets & Writers*, among others. She is currently a doctoral student in Literature & Creative Writing at the University of Houston.

TOLBERT SMALL

is known as the Peoples Doctor or the Doctors Doctor and did house calls throughout the flatlands of Oakland. He was one of the first acupuncturists in the disunited states. He was the physician for the Black Panthers. including Angela Davis and George Jackson. He believes poetry, like medícine belongs to the people and should serve the people.

JOHN SIMS

John Sims, a Detroit native, is a polymath artist, writer, and activist who creates art and curatorial multimedia projects informed by mathematics, design, the politics of white supremacy, sacred symbols/anniversaries, and poetic/political text. For 20 years, he has been working on the forefront of contemporary mathematical art and leading the national pushback on Confederate iconography. www.johnsimsprojects.com

LANDON SMITH

lives in Oakland, California, and processes the world through poetry. He has been published in various publications in 2020. He believes real poetry is concerned with impact, and that is his goal—impact. He hopes his words are merely the vessel for something larger.

MIMI TEMPESTT

I'm originally from Los Angeles, and when I moved to Oakland and drove down International for the first time, I was reminded of certain streets (as well the stories of Black women I know) in Downtown LA where I grew up. It seems that no matter what metropolis Black women find ourselves in, we all face similar circumstances.

COVER ART MISSIVE

On "African American Pi"

BY THE ARTIST, JOHN SIMS

From bee hives to social revolution, the rhythm of structure moves fluidly across the elements of nature and culture leaving convincing evidence that mathematical vision, creative expression, and community strength are profound partners in the search for truth, justice and survival.

"African American Pi" is a quilt that visualizes in base three, in the red, black and red, the beginning part of the irrational circle constant Pi, as a metaphor for locating one's space, one's home, one's community in the complicated aperiodic Circle of separations and suppression. This work is a part of a system of 13 quilts featured in "SquareRoots: A Quilted Manifesto," a multimedia project that explores Pythagorean mathematics, African textiles, and the visualization of the Pi in various bases, the different faces of irrationality, visual equations, digital portraiture, and the ordering of native African designs from both Ghana and central Africa. Each quilt is associated with a co-quilt—with all of the quilts forming the conceptual collective HyperQuilts whose co-quilt is the central African quilt.

NOMADIC PRESS
BLACK WRITERS FUND

NOMADIC PRESS
EMERGENCY FUND

OTHER WAYS TO SUPPORT NOMADIC PRESS' WRITERS

In 2020, two funds geared specifically toward supporting our writers were created: the **Nomadic Press Black Writers Fund** and the **Nomadic Press Emergency Fund.**

The former is a forever fund that puts money directly into the pockets of our Black writers. The latter provides up to $200 dignity-centered emergency grants to any of our writers in need.

Please consider supporting these funds. You can also more generally support Nomadic Press by donating to our general fund via nomadicpress.org/donate and by continuing to buy our books. As always, thank you for your support!

Scan here for more information and/or to donate.
You can also donate at nomadicpress.org/store.